Tempo Books
14

Happy Christmas

Paul Groves and Leslie Stratta

Illustrated by Robert Tavener

Longman

1 Dad Goes to School

"Come on," said Dad, "hurry up!"
It was Saturday. They were going to take Gran for a
spin and go shopping.
"I won't be a minute," said Linda, "I've just got
this button to sew on."
"Not you," said Dad. "You've got your homework
to do. I want it done this week-end, not like last."

"Dad, I want to come shopping."
"You were up till twelve on Sunday night to finish it.
I'm not having that again."
"Mum," said Linda.
"Your father's right," said Mum.
"I hate school," exclaimed Linda. "I wish it had
never been invented."
"You don't know how well off you are," said Dad.
"I'd give my back teeth to be back at school. Come
on. Mum."
"All right, I'm ready," said Mum.

As Dad came up to the traffic lights they changed to
red. "Just the day for a bit of a spin," he said. "Don't
spend too long shopping."
"You can't hurry Gran," said Mum.

"The car's running well," said Dad.

"It should do. It cost enough to have it repaired last time," Mum replied.

"Yes," said Dad," I don't want another bill like that one."

The lights changed to green and Dad drove off quickly along the road. He turned into the High Street and stopped at a zebra crossing. People began to cross. Dad tapped on the wheel. "Come on," he said.

"Don't be in such a hurry," said Mum.

As the last person crossed Dad drove off again. The High Street was full of traffic. People were doing their week-end shopping.

Just as Dad was coming to the end of the High Street the car began to jerk and shudder, and then stopped.

"Oh no!" exclaimed Mum.

Dad swore under his breath and turned the key. The
engine started and they drove off again. "Thank God
for that," said Dad. He turned off the High Street on
his way to the car park. At that moment the car
began to jerk again and shudder. Then it stopped
right on a corner.

"Oh, not again," said Mum.
Dad turned the key again, but this time the engine
would not start. Dad began to sweat. He kept turning
the key. The engine still would not start. Cars were
piling up behind and their drivers were pressing
their horns.
"Try again," said Mum.
"It's no good; it's dead," yelled Dad. "What a place
to break down!"

He got out of the car and with two other men pushed the car into the kerb. Mum sat in it feeling very silly as people stared.

Dad went into a shop and asked if he could phone the garage. Then he went back and stood by the car. A traffic warden came up. "Are you going to move this?" he asked. "There's a queue the whole length of the High Street." Mum got out and they pushed it partly onto the pavement.

After a long while a truck came and towed Dad's car away. It was a broken fan belt. Dad and Mum had to go to Gran's by bus to explain what had happened. "I thought you knew all about cars," said Gran.

"He doesn't," said Mum.

"It could happen to anybody," said Dad.

Two days later Dad picked up the car from the garage. They gave him the bill. Dad gasped. "What's this?" he exclaimed.

"Well, mate," said the man, "If you don't want to pay big bills you shouldn't break down on a Saturday afternoon. The service department is shut then. I had to get a bloke from home to tow you in."

"Anyone would think you used a Rolls," grumbled Dad. He drove off very angry.

Dad went on about the bill for two days. The family got fed up with it. On Thursday Linda came home from school with a leaflet. She gave it to Dad.

"What's this?" asked Dad.

"Read it," said Linda.

"Evening classes?" said Dad. "What do I want this for?"

"Look at page four," Linda told him.

"Repair your own car," read Dad. "A course of
twenty classes on the care of your car."
"Yes," said Linda, "if you're so worried about big
car bills, do your own repairs and servicing."
"What a good idea," said Mum wiping her hands.
"Let me see."
"You can sign on tonight,"
said Linda.
"Well . . .," mumbled Dad.
"I don't want to break down
in the High Street
again," said Mum.
"Well . . .," mumbled Dad.
"I wish I could do it,"
said Jim coming in.
"All right," said Dad,
"I'll go."

It was some weeks later. Dad was looking at the *TV
Times*. He settled back in the arm chair. "There's a
good evening's telly on tonight," he said. He lit his
pipe and lay back.
"There may be," said Mum, "but you're not
watching it."
"Why?" asked Dad. His pipe dropped in his mouth.
"It's your evening class."
"Oh," said Dad. "I'm a bit tired tonight. I thought
I might give it a miss."
"You said you would give your back teeth to go back
to school," said Linda.

"So I would," said Dad, "but I've done a day's work."
"Come on," said Mum. She brought in his coat.
"Well I was supposed to do a bit of writing for this week and . . ."
"And you've spent the last two evenings down at the pub."
"And you tell me about my homework!" exclaimed Linda.
"Come on," said Mum. "We've paid out good money for these classes and you're not going to miss any."
"Oh, all right," said Dad.

Mum and Linda heard him slam the door. Then they both started to laugh. They laughed so much Jim came in to see what was so funny on the television.

2 April Fool

The lads were camping at Grandad's. Ted leapt out
of the tent. "It's snowing!" he yelled.
"No," said Jim.
"It is!" yelled Ted.
Jim and the others jumped out of their sleeping bags.
"It's not!" they cried.
"Ha! Ha! April Fool!" yelled Ted. "It's the first
of April. Got you."
"I forgot," said Jim. "But you won't forget this. A
pinch and a punch for the first day of the month."
He chased Ted and punched him.

The lads cooked breakfast. "Your shoelace is undone,"
said Mick to Ted.
"You can't catch me," said Ted. "I was up before
you."

The lads tried to catch Ted. Cliff said there was a
rat behind him. Jim said his Mum wanted him on
the phone in the farm. But he could not be caught.
He was full of himself. "I know," he said, "let's
catch Grandad."
"How?" asked Jim. "He's clever, your Grandad."
"Something to do with his pigs. He won't suspect
that," said Ted.
"We could say one was ill," Cliff put in.
"No, he'll have looked at them this morning," said
Ted. "I know let's say the sty is on fire."
"Yes, that will get him," cried Mick.

"Fire! Fire! Fire!" The lads run up to the farm banging on a frying pan.

Grandad runs out. "Where?" he cries.

"The pig sties!" yells Ted.

"I'll get some water," says Grandad.

The lads turn away so he cannot see them laughing. Soon he staggers up to the pig sties with two buckets of water.

"Help me get some more!" he cries. Then he stops.

"Where's the fire?" he says.

"April Fool!" yell the lads.

"April Fool?" says Grandad.

"It's April Fools' Day, Grandad," Ted tells him.

"You blooming lads. You had me worried then."

Grandad is not pleased at the joke. He growls and

goes back to the house.

Later the lads go on a bike ride. They think it best
to get out of Grandad's way for the day as he is still
cross with them. But when they get back at seven
Grandad is at the gate to meet them. "Had a good
day?" he asks.

"Yes," they tell him. "We're starving."

"I thought you would be. As a treat I've got a big
supper for you."

"Smashing," says Ted.

"He's a good sport your Grandad," says Cliff.

"One of the best," says Ted.

Grandad has made a big steak and kidney pie. He
gives the lads big helpings of potatoes, peas and the
pie. They tuck in and they are soon wiping their
plates clean with some fresh bread Grandad has
baked.

"Had enough?" asks Grandad.

"Well . . ." says Ted.

"Say no more," says Grandad. He gives Ted a second
helping of pie.

Ted leans back very full up. "That was a good supper, Grandad."

"Well, I wanted you to sleep well," says Grandad. "A good meal helps."

"We always sleep well except on the first night," Ted tells him.

"Yes, but I wanted you to sleep well tonight."

"Why tonight?"

"Well, it's the night of the ghost."

"Oh, you're always trying to fool me with that story about a ghost walking at night," says Ted.

Grandad sits and looks at the fire. He takes out his pipe. "It's true," he says.

"Tell us about it," says Mick.

"Well, do you believe in ghosts?" asks Grandad.
"No," says Ted.
"I do," says Jim.
"They do say one walks here tonight."
"That's a load of rubbish," exclaims Ted.
"How do you think I got this place? Got it cheap because no one else would have it. Because of the ghost." Grandad pulls on his pipe.
"Tell us, Grandad," says Cliff.

"Well, if you're sure it won't stop you from sleeping." Grandad stared into the fire. "Back in 1856 a young man who lived here was jilted by a girl. Women, you see. Always make trouble, women. He'd played an April Fool trick on her and she upped and left him. So come midnight he drowned himself in the canal."
"What happened then?" asked Jim.
"Every April Fool night after that, the ghost of the man is seen near the canal at midnight," says Grandad.

"Have you seen it, Grandad?" asks Cliff.
"I'm not saying. Might upset you. They do say he walks out of the farm door, down through the field past the sties, past your tents and throws himself into the canal."

"That's rubbish," says Ted. "You're always trying to fool me, Grandad."
"Well, have a good night. By the way, did you enjoy those snails?" asks Grandad.
"Snails?" exclaims Ted.
"Yes, I put some snails in the pie to give it flavour."
"Snails!" says Ted. His mouth is open.
"Yes, some fat Sussex snails like my old Granny did in her pies. Did you like them?"
"Ugh!" says Mick.

"I only put in ten," says Grandad. "Sleep well. I'm
off to bed."
Ted begins to look sick.

The lads are in the tent
trying to sleep. Ted is
groaning. "I feel sick. Those snails!"
"I do a bit too," adds Mick.
"Go to sleep," says Jim.
"The French eat them."
"I'm English," groans Ted.
"What time is it?" asks Cliff.
"It's nearly midnight," Jim tells him.
"Time for the ghost," says Cliff.
"Let's look out," says Jim.
"No," says Ted.

"I thought you didn't believe in ghosts?" Jim says.
"I don't but I don't feel like looking out," Ted replies.
"A bit of a walk would do you good."
"No."
"I'll take a look," says Cliff. He gets up and goes out
of the tent. "Here look!" he calls back. "There's
something white near the farm."
"You're pulling my leg," says Ted.
"Come and look."
Ted slowly gets out of bed, groaning. He looks over
towards the farm. "There is," he says.
"It's coming this way," whispers Jim. All of the lads
are out of the tent by now. They watch hardly
breathing.

"It's coming closer," says Cliff.

"I'm getting out of here," says Ted.

The lads run away but Ted trips over a guy rope. "Wait for me!" he yells. A hand grips him as he gets up. "Help, save me!" he cries.

"What's up?" says Grandad. "I've just brought some extra blankets as it's turned so cold tonight." He is standing there with them round his shoulders. The top one is white.

"Grandad!" gasps Ted.

"Who else were you expecting?"

"We thought you were the ghost."

"You don't believe in that rubbish, do you?"

"But you told us . . ."

"More April Fool you then."

"That's not fair. April Fools' day stops at twelve midday."

"No more fair to pretend my pig sty was on fire. A silly thing to do. I thought I would teach you a lesson."

"You didn't have to put snails in the pie as well," says Ted.

"You don't think I would ruin a good steak and kidney pie with snails do you?"

"Grandad!"

The lads have come back. "It will be a long time before you play a trick on Grandad again," they tell Ted.

3   Hole in One

Jim is on the common. He has an old golf club he
found in a junk shop. He is hitting a golf ball and Gus
is helping him to find it. Gus thinks it is great fun.
Jim has had some lessons at school and he thinks he
might take up the game one day. He is finding it
difficult to hit the ball straight.

Ted comes up on his bike. "What are you doing?" he
asks.

"Drilling for oil," says Jim.

"I thought you were," says Ted. "All those big holes
you have dug trying to hit that little ball."

"You try," says Jim. "It's not easy."

"Simple game. I've seen it on the telly. All you have to do is get that little ball in a big hole. I do better on the putting green in the park than they do on the telly."

"Have a go," suggests Jim.

"Right," agrees Ted. He has a big swipe at the ball and misses. "Just getting my eye in," he explains. He has another go and misses. "Funny club, this," he says. He has one more swipe and the ball curls away into a clump of gorse bushes.

"You fool!" yells Jim. "Now you've lost it and it's my only ball."

"Gus will find it," says Ted.

But Gus cannot find it. They all hunt in the bushes. Jim gets cross with Ted.

20

"My Dad has some old clubs he never uses now," says
Ted. "I'll ask him to lend them to me. I'll play you
on a real course."
"O.K.," says Jim.
They go back to the flats.

The next day Ted calls for Jim with the clubs. They
get them out of the bag and look at them.
"Not bad," says Jim.
"Let's play this afternoon," suggests Ted.
"It's expensive," Jim tells him.
"I've got plenty of money," says Ted. "And it's
worth it to give you a beating."

Linda is looking at the clubs. "Can I come?" she asks.
"Not to play!" exclaims Ted.
"Women do play; I've seen them."
"Yes, but . . ."
"Don't get worried. I only want to watch," she says.
"You can come if you carry the clubs," says Jim.
"You can be my caddie," adds Ted.
"I don't mind," says Linda.

At the golf course the man looks at the one bag of clubs. "I shouldn't let you on here with only one bag," he says.

"Please let us, mister," pleads Ted. "We've come a long way."

"All right," says the man, "it's not too busy today. But don't hold up any other players."

Jim, Ted and Linda go to the first tee. The green is four hundred metres away.

"I'll do this in three," says Ted. "Two to the green and one putt."

"That's called a birdie," says Jim.

"Why?" asks Linda.

"I don't know," says Jim.

Ted swings at the ball and misses. He has another swing and misses again. "Tricky course this," he remarks.

"That's two," says Jim. "You said you would do it in three. You've got to hole this shot."

"What do you mean? I didn't hit the ball."

"They all count."

Linda laughs.

Ted is very cross. He has a big swipe at the ball. It goes off the toe of the club, nearly hits Linda and goes into a clump of bushes.

"You've lost that," says Jim.

"I'll find it," says Ted.

"See you on the green then." Jim drives off and goes into a sand bunker. It takes him two to get out and then four more shots to the green. When he is putting Ted runs up.

"You didn't help me," he complains.
"The man said not to hold up other people and there
are some behind us," Jim tells him.
"What about you?"
"I'm not laddering my tights in there," says Linda.
"You're my caddie," says Ted.
"I didn't expect to have to look for balls," said Linda.

They go to the next tee. There is a pond in front of
it. "How lovely!" exclaims Linda.
"Not so lovely when you've got to drive across it,"
says Jim.
"Child's play," says Ted.
Jim drives off. "Plop!" goes the ball into the pond.
Ted rolls about laughing. Then he has a go. "Plop!"
Now it is Jim's and Linda's turn to laugh.
"I don't see what's so funny," says Ted.
Jim drives off again and gets over. So does Ted and

his ball goes past Jim's. They run after their golf balls
leaving Linda to carry the clubs.
Jim takes his next shot and it goes into a bunker.

"You didn't get to the green!" yells Ted. "Watch
this!" He takes a big swipe. The ball starts off straight
but then curls away into some house gardens by the
course.
"Another lost ball," says Jim. "And you may have
killed somebody." They run to the next tee.
"Now we've only one ball left," says Jim. "We
started with five."
"You can watch me then," says Ted.
"No!" yells Jim.
Linda comes up. "You could have waited for me,"
she says. "What are you quarrelling about?"
"We've only one ball left," says Jim.
"Right," says Linda, "as you've both been so rotten
you can let me play this one."

"Girls can't play golf!" exclaims Ted.
"I can't do worse than you," Linda tells him.
"All right," says Jim.
"Cor!" says Ted.

They go to the ladies' tee. This is a short hole. They can see the green not far away. Jim shows Linda how to grip the club.
"It does feel funny," she says. Then she takes a big swing. The ball goes up in the air, drops on the green, runs across it, hits the flag stick and drops in the hole.
"A hole in one!" yells Jim.
"Fluke," says Ted.
"What an easy game," says Linda. "I don't know why you two have been making so much fuss about it."
"I'm going home," says Ted.

4 *Sandra*

Jim was just coming out of Mr Bates' shop when
Sandra came in. "Hello, stranger," she said.
"Lo," said Jim. He had not seen much of Sandra
lately.
"Going back to the flats?" she asked.
"Yeh," said Jim.
"I'll come with you. I want to see Linda."
Jim waited, flicking through some magazines, while
Sandra got the paper for her Dad and some mints for
her Gran.
"The prices of these sweets," she said.
"Yeh, it costs a lot to get rotten teeth these days,"
said Jim.

Later they were walking back down the High Street. The dustmen had been on strike and rubbish was piled high in front of some of the shops. Sandra suddenly slipped on a piece of orange peel. Jim grabbed her before she fell. Sandra hung on to him until they got to the end of the street. "Thanks," she said. "My Dad would put this lot in prison. It's disgusting."

"They don't get paid that much," said Jim. He did not really want to have an argument with Sandra but he had to speak his mind.
Sandra suddenly looked at him straight in the eyes. "Do you think my Dad is wrong then?" she asked.
Jim blushed. "It's a rotten job. I just think the

dustmen have a case that's all." Girls could get so upset in an argument.

"Where have you been lately?" she asked. "I don't seem to have seen so much of you. You're either with the boys or off to Ted's Grandad's or playing cricket."

"Yeh, I've been busy," said Jim. "You know how it is."

"I used to like talking to you," said Sandra.

"I talk to you at the club," he said. Girls could get so personal.

"There's all those others there," said Sandra. "I expect there's some other girl you like."

Jim felt the blush this time, deep in his face. "No, there's no other girl," he said. "I just get so busy and there's all that homework."

"I have homework to do too," said Sandra.

"Ouch!" Jim jumped. Cliff and Ted had come up behind him and Ted had thumped him on the back. "Give over, Ted," said Jim. "That hurt."
"Didn't see us," grinned Ted.

"Yeh, you were talking too much. We've been watching you," said Cliff.
"Just talking about homework," Jim told them.
"Ugh!" exclaimed Ted. "Don't mention that word at the week-end."
"Don't forget the cricket this afternoon on the common," said Cliff. "The match I fixed up with the Southfields lot."

30

"I'm playing," said Ted.

"Not with my bat," Jim told him.

"He can have mine," said Cliff. "See you at two. We must go and see Mr Atkins about some stumps. Come on, Ted."

"So long," said Ted. "Enjoy your talk about . . . ugh . . . I can't bring myself to say the word."

"I'd better be going too," said Sandra.

"I thought you wanted to see Linda," exclaimed Jim.

"That can wait." She tossed her blonde hair and it fanned over her shoulder.

Jim hesitated. Then he said, "Why not come and watch the cricket?"

"I'd rather play," said Sandra.

"Cliff doesn't like girls in the team. It'll be a tough match. They'll bowl fast."

"So what."

"So you might get hurt."

"That wouldn't worry you," Sandra said.

"Of course it would." As he said it he really meant it.

"I'll come and watch then," said Sandra, "though I'd still rather play."

"Good shot, Cliff!" Jim clapped. The sun was hot on the common.

"Almost as good as I can hit," said Ted.

"I can't get comfortable," said Sandra. She leaned against her arm and stretched out on the grass. Her hair spilled over her shoulders. "That's better."

Jim liked Sandra being there. It made him feel sort of pleasant. Glad to be alive watching cricket. The hot sun making his skin tacky. He would like to be on his own sometimes with her, without the gang being there. He would show her how he could play. He would go in and score a quick fifty runs.

"Click!" Cliff's middle stump came out.
"Cliff's out," said Ted. "In you go."
"Good luck," said Sandra, giving him a pat on the back.
"Thanks," said Jim.

"Watch that coloured boy," said Cliff. "The ball shoots through low sometimes."
He would. He felt confident and glanced back at the team before he faced the first ball.
Once the ball pitched it never lifted; it went under his bat and broke the wicket. He was out for a duck. He walked back jabbing his bat in the ground.
Sandra looked very sorry for him. "Bad luck, Jim," she said.
"I did warn you," said Cliff.
"Nobody could've touched that ball," said Jim. He flung his bat down and sprawled on the grass. He felt such a fool.

That fool Ted was scoring runs as Cliff and the rest of
the team jumped up and down, giving advice. Jim
was now sitting alone with Sandra. "Come on, Jim,
cheer up," she said "It's not the end of the world."
Jim began to feel better. "Let's go for a walk and
watch from the other side for a while," he said.
"Yes, come on, a walk will cheer you up."
Jim felt a lot better as they walked away. He clapped
Ted who had just hit a six. He liked being with
Sandra. He must try and see more of her at the club.
"Penny for your thoughts," she said.
He felt himself starting to blush. "I was just thinking
what a nice day it was," he said.

5　Happy Christmas

It is Christmas Day. All the family is sitting round looking at their presents. Gran is with them. She has knitted presents for them all: a hat for Jim to keep him warm on his paper round; gloves for Linda; a pullover for Dad; and bed socks for Mum.

"This is the life," says Dad. He puts down his glass of whisky and puffs on a big cigar Jim has given him. "Is the turkey in yet?"

"It's been in over an hour," Mum tells him. "We can't all sit back on Christmas Day."

"It's not one of those frozen ones, I hope," says Gran. "No taste in them. Not much taste in any food these days."

"No, it's not," Mum tells her. "It's a fresh one from the market."

"I got it," says Dad. "So you can blame me if it's not a good one."

"I wish it was Christmas Day every day," says Jim. He has a mouthful of sweets. "Don't eat too many of those," says Mum, "or you won't want any turkey."

"Do you think I made the stuffing right?" asks Linda. "Of course you did, dear," Mum tells her.

The family is sitting round the table. Dad has poured them out a glass of wine each. "Bring in the turkey!" he shouts, holding up the carving knife.

In the kitchen Mum has just got it out of the oven. "I
hope it's been in long enough," she says.
"It looks lovely and brown," says Linda.
"Yes, I think it's just right," says Mum.
"Come on!" Dad calls.
"We're waiting," says Jim.
"Hark at them in there. You'd think they hadn't
eaten for a week," exclaims Linda.
"I think your Dad's drunk too much," says Mum.
"He'll be ill tomorrow if he doesn't watch it."
Gran comes into the kitchen. "Is it all right?" she
asks.
"Yes," says Mum. "Now sit down and Linda and I
will bring it in."

Linda proudly comes in with the turkey. "Hooray!"
says Dad.
"Don't drop it," says Jim.
"I hope you'll think of all the starving people in the
world when you eat this," Mum remarks.
"Just let me get my teeth into it," says Dad.

It is afternoon. The television is on. Jim and Dad
are almost asleep. Mum, Linda and Gran have just
finished the washing up. "Right," says Mum, "time
for a walk."

"A what?" asks Dad.

"A walk. I want you to go out for a walk on the common so I can clear up and have a little rest. I've been on my feet all morning."

"But it's cold out," says Dad.

"Just what you need after all that stuffing. You can wear Gran's new pullover to keep you warm. Come on, Jim, and take this dog with you."

"Me as well?" asks Jim.

"Yes, you as well. You've got your nice woolly hat to put on."

"Come on," urges Linda, "it'll do us all good. We can give the ducks their Christmas dinner as well."

Dad, Linda and Jim set off across the common. There are not many people about. They go to the windmill and then down to the pond.

Linda feeds the ducks with some old bread. Suddenly Gus barks at something under a bush. "What is it, boy?" says Jim. "Oh!"

"What is it?" asks Linda.

"It's a duck," says Jim.

"I think it's hurt."

Dad comes to look.

The duck looks very sick. "It's wing is broken," says Dad.

"Poor thing," sighs Linda.

"At Christmas too."

"What can we do?" asks Jim.

"We can't leave it here," says Linda. "A dog will get it. Let's take it home and get the RSPCA."

Linda takes the duck back to the flat. Gus keeps jumping up at it. "Down, boy," yells Jim.
"What is it?" asks Mum.
"We found it on the common. It's broken its wing."
"Poor thing," says Gran.
"I'll phone the RSPCA from Mrs Jenkins," says Linda.

Linda comes back. "The man can't come yet. He says keep it warm in a box."
Mum gets a box and puts the duck in it with one of Dad's old pullovers.

The family sits round watching television. Linda looks sad. Mum looks sad. Gran looks sad.
"This is a real happy Christmas," says Dad.
"Well, how can we be happy with that poor thing in the kitchen?" asks Linda. She keeps getting up to look at it. It looks very sick. Its eyes are running.
"It's only a duck," says Dad. "Have a drink and forget about it."

Teatime comes. "I'm not hungry," says Linda.
"I don't think I am," agrees Mum.
"Just a cup of tea for me," adds Gran.
"It's not going to spoil my tea," says Dad. "I enjoy it when we pull the crackers and read out all those daft jokes."
"You and Jim can," says Mum.
"What a Christmas!" says Dad. "A real happy Christmas. All because of a duck."

Christmas tea is a sad meal. Later in the evening Linda comes into the lounge from the kitchen. "Oh," she says, "I think it's dead."
"Let me see," says Mum and goes into the kitchen. "Yes, it is."
They both cry. Gran comes in and cries as well. Jim

follows her out and wants to cry as well but holds
back the tears.

"What a happy Christmas," complains Dad as he
too comes into the kitchen.

"The poor thing; have you no feelings?" asks Mum.

"Feelings!" exclaims Dad. "You've spent the morning
worrying if you had roasted one bird properly. Now
you expect me to worry about one that's died in a
normal way."

"That's different," says Linda.

"Different," says Dad. "Your stomach's full of bird."
Tears roll down Linda's face.

"Women!" says Dad. "What a lovely way to spend
Christmas Day." He goes back into the lounge, pours
himself a whisky and lights another cigar. "Happy
Christmas," he says to Gus as he sits down again to
watch the television.

Word List

DAD GOES TO SCHOOL

Long Vowel 'ur'
jerk	Saturday
kerb	Thursday
person	turned
work	turning
homework	

Diphthong Vowel 'ear'
idea

Diphthong Vowel 'air'
chair
repair
repaired
care
stared
there's

Triphthong Vowel 'ire'
tired

'er' endings
after(noon)
corner
father
never
shudder

'le' endings
grumble(d)
mumble(d)
settle(d)

Words of 3 Syllables
department
invented

Soft 'c'
place
service
servicing

Soft 'g'
engine
garage

Abbreviations
can't
doesn't
don't
I'd
I've
shouldn't
there's
we've
you're
you've

Other Words
another	money
anybody	move
anyone	people
break	phone
breath	piling
brought	queue
change	ready
changed	school
course	sew
dead	sweat
done	these
enough	thought
evening	tonight
four	warden
key	watching
laugh	worried
laughed	would
minute	writing

APRIL FOOL

Long Vowel 'ur'
first

Diphthong Vowel 'ear'
near
nearly

Diphthong Vowel 'air'
fair
stared

Diphthong Vowel 'oi'
boys
enjoy

Diphthong Vowel 'oor'
sure

Triphthong Vowel 'ire'
fire

'er' endings
after
clever
closer
ever(y)
later
staggers
suffer
whispers

Words of 3 Syllables
every
expecting

Soft 'c'
except

Abbreviations
can't
don't
he'd
he'll
he's
I'll
I'm
it's
I've
let's
we're
won't
you're

Other Words

always	ghost	through
April	guy	tonight
because	kidney	towards
believe	laughing	trouble
bread	leapt	true
breakfast	month	thought
brought	potatoes	undone
caught	pulling	water
English	pulls	wiping
enough	ruin	women
field	shoelace	worried
flavour	shoulders	would
full	something	young
	steak	

HOLE IN ONE

Long Vowel 'ur'
laddering
first
girls
worth
curls

Diphthong Vowel 'ear'
nearly

Diphthong Vowel 'oi'
oil

'er' endings   *'le' endings*
after(noon)   little
better   simple
bunker
mister
never
players

Words of 3 Syllables
difficult
expensive
laddering
quarrelling

Soft 'g'
suggests

Abbreviations
can't
didn't
don't
I'll
it's
I've
let's
shouldn't
we've
you're
you've

Other Words

another	lovely
birdie	metres
busy	money
caddie	people
course	somebody
does	straight
eye	thought
fluke	today
four	toe
goes	watch
great	women
ladies	worried
laughing	
laughs	

SANDRA

Long Vowel 'ur'
personal
first
girls
word
homework
world
hurt

Diphthong Vowel 'u'
used

Diphthong Vowel 'ear'
cheer

Diphthong Vowel 'air'
hair

'er' endings
after(noon)
better
later
never
paper
rather
under

'le' endings
middle

Words of 3 Syllables
confident
disgusting
personal
suddenly

Words of 4 Syllables
hesitated

Soft 'c'
advice
face
faced
glanced
nice
prices

Soft 'g'
orange

Abbreviations
could've
didn't
doesn't
don't
I'd
I'll
it'll
it's
let's
that's
they'll
we've
wouldn't

Other Words

almost	pleasant
argument	shoulders
busy	sometimes
coloured	Southfields
comfortable	straight
course	stranger
either	these
eyes	though
front	thoughts
magazines	tough
making	warn
meant	watch
mention	watching
nobody	worry
once	would
piece	

HAPPY CHRISTMAS

Long Vowel 'ur'
bird
world
hurt
turkey

Diphthong Vowel 'u'
new

Diphthong Vowel 'ear'
clear
tears

Diphthong Vowel 'air'
wear

Diphthong Vowel 'oi'
boy
enjoy

Diphthong Vowel 'oor'
pour(ed)
pours

Triphthong Vowel 'our'
(h)our

'er' endings
after(noon)
crackers
differ(ent)
dinner
ever(y)
later
paper
proper(ly)

'le' endings
little

Words of 3 Syllables
different
every
properly
suddenly

Soft 'c'
cigar

Soft 'g'
lounge
urges

Abbreviations

can't	we're
doesn't	won't
don't	you'd
hadn't	you'll
he'll	you've
I'll	
it'll	
it's	
I've	

Other Words

almost	pullover
because	something
bread	stomach
bush	table
Christmas	taste
course	television
enough	these
evening	tomorrow
eyes	warm
full	washing
gloves	watch
lovely	watching
many	women
people	worry
phone	worrying
pull	